THE
FOREST
IN OLD PHOTOGRAPHS
A SECOND SELECTION

To all who love the Forest
but especially Alex, Doreen,
Elsie, Eric, Frances, John,
Leslie and Marina

THE
FOREST
IN OLD PHOTOGRAPHS
A SECOND SELECTION

COLLECTED BY
HUMPHREY PHELPS

ALAN SUTTON
1984

Alan Sutton Publishing Limited
Brunswick Road · Gloucester

First published 1984

British Library Cataloguing in Publication Data

Phelps, Humphrey
The Forest in old photographs: a second selection
1. Forest of Dean (Gloucestershire : District)
—Social life and customs
I. Title
942.4'13082   DA670.D25

ISBN 0-86299-186-2

Typesetting and origination by
Alan Sutton Publishing Limited.
Printed in Great Britain.

CONTENTS

(Unless stated otherwise 'left' and 'right' refer to the *reader's* left or right)

'The virtue of the camera is not the power it has to transform the photographer into an artist, but the impulse it gives him to keep on looking'

Brooks Atkinson

INTRODUCTION

These photographs came from the last years of the nineteenth century and the first fifty years of this century. They are, therefore, from a period when coalmining dominated the heart of the territory covered in this collection and when coalmining itself was the heart of many places shown in these photographs.

Sometime during the nineteenth century, a Coleford man known as Jolly Jack Nash and with a considerable reputation on the London music halls, scored a hit with the song: 'We're the Jovial Foresters, our trade is getting coal.' At that time getting coal was the trade of many Foresters.

Coal had been mined in the Forest for centuries, and by the eighteenth century there was a proliferation of pits. But it was the nineteenth century which saw the advent of the large collieries; Crump Meadow, Foxes Bridge, Lightmoor, New

Bowson, New Fancy, Trafalgar, Waterloo... By 1900 the annual output of coal from the Forest was one million tons and it was estimated that there were three hundred million tons of unworked coal, most of it winnable, in Dean.

In 1874 there were five thousand colliers in the Forest, the large colliery owners built large houses. By the 1920s there were seven thousand colliers, but many of the collieries were sometimes only working one or two shifts per week. In 1955 the number had reduced to two and a half thousand, and ten years later the last big colliery closed.

Because the collieries were so much a part of the period, I have, in the coalmining section included photographs from a later date to include their end. Similarly with Forest sheep, to include the great slaughter of 1956. The sheep, also so much a part of the Forest are back; and, fortunately we still have a few Free Miners carrying on the traditional trade of getting coal.

The prices displayed in the shop windows seem absurdly low, but in 1884 the average wage of a collier was three shillings and eightpence a shift. In 1937 the top rate for a collier working under a buttyman was seven and ninepence.

It is, I think, evident in the photographs of the shops, that the Forester had little need to travel further afield for most of his needs. Almost every item, food, household goods, clothes etc., could be obtained locally, and that those enterprising local traders put supermarkets to shame. However should anyone want to travel, the railway provided the means.

This land between two rivers has so much variety that it is difficult to include every aspect of it. There are the rivers themselves; the Severn has the larger selection because it has the more interesting photographs, most obtainable of the Wye were of scenery which has scarcely changed and there was little point in including such photographs.

The farming photographs show the great and rapid change in the last thirty or forty years. The year 1950 was chosen as a convenient stopping point and because it was felt that photographs taken after that date could not really be called old. But looking through this collection I realise that 1950 was more than a convenient point, it was – give or take a few years, a dividing point.

This period saw the end of many industries which sprang out of the Forest and its resources. It saw the end of so many local trades and crafts; the miller, the wheelwright, the saddler, the shoemaker. The end of horse-power, water-power; the decline of steam-power, almost the end of railways in Dean – then there were dozens of railway stations, now there is only one. It also saw the end of much hardship and injustice. But, without wishing to glamorise the past I do suggest that this collection also shows something of that wonderful but indefinable quality that made the Forest unique.

This collection shows what we have lost, I can only hope that it may do something to make us hold fast to what customs, rights, culture and traditions remain. Tradition is a guide and not a jailer. If these photographs tell us anything, above all they tell us of the strong bond of comradeship that existed in the Forest; and if that is lost, and the pride and independence, the Forest itself will be lost.

Some photographs are undated because I did not know the exact date, but the reader will be able to place some of them by the clothes people are wearing – and if the reader is female, probably a great deal more accurately than I. Bearing in mind of course that fashion would have been slow to change in the Forest and that the Forester would not have discarded good clothes merely for the sake of fashion.

I hope these photographs will give as much pleasure as I have had in collecting them. I hope, too, that it will cause everyone to cherish what photographs they have and inspire many to take photographs today – those too will become old photographs in time and record something that may no longer be. The camera gives the impetus to keep looking. There is still plenty to look for yet in the Forest. And may I suggest black and white, not colour film?

All I have said so far is only a preamble to the tributes I want to pay to the men, women and children who made these scenes; to the photographers who took them and preserved them for us. Also to express my gratitude to those who have preserved the photographs and have been kind enough to loan them, and to so many who have told me so much that I did not know. Although it is my name which appears upon the cover, this book is really their book.

SECTION ONE

Round and About

'Variety is the soul of pleasure'
Aphra Behn

BLAISDON. The Tanhouse, August 1906. Mrs Hill and two daughters. The name of the house commemorates the existence of a tannery in the eighteenth century. The house was faced in brick c. 1800. John Dowding who discovered the Blaisdon Red Plum lived here during the latter part of the nineteenth century.

BLAKENEY, early twentieth century. 'The village of Blakeney is pleasantly water'd by a lively stream' (John Byng, 1781). The King's Head is an eighteenth century building. The large building was Butler's shop which sold grocery and all kinds of things. The building beside it was Butler's corn-mill. On this stretch of the stream, which was soon to be covered, horses used to be watered and traps were washed.

BLAKENEY. Shoemaker's shop, 1901. In 1901 Blakeney had three shoemakers – these premises were later occupied by Frederick Baldwin, another shoemaker – six grocers, two butchers, two millers, four public houses, two blacksmiths and two wheelwrights. There were fairs held in the street, in May and November. This photograph and the next one are part of a series taken by R.A. Malby and H.W. Sivell who spent a holiday at Blakeney, Easter, 1901.

BLAKENEY. The Tump Inn, 1901. The shed contained a cider mill.

BREAM. The Sun Tump. Someone has written 1900 on the photograph, but the telegraph pole and the notice 'You may telephone from here' suggest a later date. In 1900, a Charles Morse was at the Oakwood Mill Inn and Albert Long Ellesmore at the Sun. The brewer's dray belonged to Arnold Perrett who had a brewery at Lydney and had also taken over the old brewery premises at Blakeney.

BREAM. High Street (Maypole End), c. 1945. Within a few years the New Inn was to close; later this fine building was restored with loving care by Melville Watts, and more recently it has become part of the Dean Heritage Museum Trust. In the photograph Mr Cannock is sitting on the window-sill of his shop. Stansfield tobacco is advertised on a window blind. Most Forest colliers rolled their own cigarettes and the strong Stansfield was very popular.

CINDERFORD. Town Hall and High Street, c. 1910. Barber's shop, right. The town hall was the property of the Cinderford Co-operative Society.

CINDERFORD. Commercial Street, c. 1910. The new bank, Capital and Counties (right), and another barber's shop. Milk floats with churns – the man in gaiters chatting to the man in a float is probably the second milkman. Milk would have been dipped out of the churns with measures into customers' jugs. Unless the milk in the churns was kept well stirred the first customers got most of the cream, so the prudent milkman carried a plunger. Someone is riding a horse down the street and a horse-van is waiting outside a shop. Have the boys stopped on their way to school in order to be 'in the picture'? Boys appear to have a greater desire, or perhaps ability, than girls to be photographed.

13

CINDERFORD. Lower High Street, 1911. On the right, feeding troughs are being unloaded at Wilce and Jenkins, ironmongers, timber, oil and paint merchants, hay and straw dealers.

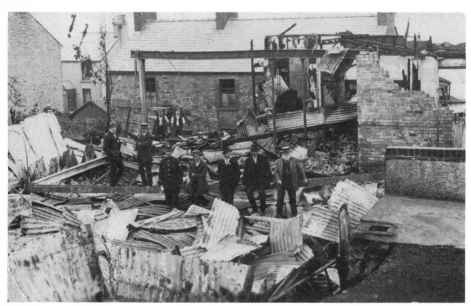

CINDERFORD. Remains of the Empire Theatre, Commercial Street, burnt down on the evening of 6 July 1919.

CINDERFORD. Market Street, 1920. Left: Kear and Sons, bakers; Whittle, grocer; Mundy, barber; also Gadd, wallpaper and paints, and above, Gore Boodle, dentist. The Misses Boud, sweets and tobacco – 'a high-class shop' said Leonard Clark who was taught music by one of the sisters; he wrote at length and with affection about the two sisters in Green Wood (published by Dobson). On the corner, India and China, grocery. On the other corner the Bon Marche, drapery, kept by Miss Cutting. There was also a coffee house in this street. Right: Samuel Rowlinson, boots and shoes.

CINDERFORD. The Swan, decorated for the coronation of Edward VII. In the foreground, Mrs Runicles and daughter Frances. Photographed by Albert Runicles of Cinderford.

COLEFORD. Market Place with the Market Hall centre. Charles II granted Coleford a Market Charter with provision for two annual fairs. The fairs were on 20th June and 24th November for the sale of wool, horses and cattle. A weekly market was held here on Fridays.

COLEFORD. View of the Market or Town Hall from the opposite direction. Tower of Coleford's original church, built 1821, restored 1862, and demolished 1882.

COLEFORD. Newland Street – Coleford was once in the parish of Newland. Left: the Baptist Chapel, Coleford was the principle Baptist town in Dean. A silk works was somewhere in this street in the early nineteenth century.

COLEFORD, High Street, 1906. Nathan Rosen, clothier, is on the left in the Market Place.

DRYBROOK, The Cross. The Royal Oak, date unknown. Two little girls have managed to get to the fore – note their leggings and the boys' knickerbockers. Behind The Royal Oak, the blacksmith's shop. Smith's baker's cart (centre) and Frank Butt's bicycle shop (left).

FLAXLEY. Waldron Farmhouse, 1907. Mr and Mrs A. Teague, daughter Vera, and Elsie Young. Under the road, not many yards from where the photographer must have stood, are the remains of the dam wall and race of the Lower Forge (eighteenth-century) where Mr Teague stored his mangolds.

GUNN'S MILL, Abenhall, c. 1905. An iron furnace, rebuilt in 1683. c. 1700 there were two corn-mills and a fulling-mill. c. 1730 the iron furnace was converted to paper-mills and paper was still being made at Gunn's Mill at the beginning of the century. The top storey of the house shown here was later removed – course by course, it is said, without removing the roof.

HAWTHORNS (HOARTHORNS), DRYBROOK, 1910. Taken from the top of the railway tunnel. Back, right centre, is Euroclydon, built by the Brain family. The tower is said to have been built so that they could see their colliery, Trafalgar. A typical Forest scene. Front left, limestone quarry, with kilns above, and railway to Mitcheldean Road Station which trains never reached by this line. Top left is now the site of the present quarry.

LITTLEDEAN, 1913, with a carrier's wagon just coming round the corner. Note: small front wheels for a good lock. The man in shirt-sleeves appears to be holding a jug.

LITTLEDEAN, Main Street. Beyond, The George and a group of trees; cottages with stable-type doors which the women leant on to gossip were known as 'ship's yud row'. Why, I wonder, did the wall (right) have to be demolished?

LYDBROOK. Lower Lydbrook and Railway Viaduct. Built in 1872 by the Cromlin Viaduct Works Company of wrought iron girders, one-hundred-and-twenty to one-hundred-and-fifty feet, spanning masonry piers ninety feet high. Speed over the viaduct was limited to 6 m.p.h. Demolished c. 1966.

LYDNEY, The Cross, c. 1925. Fourteenth-century preaching cross; the shrine on top of steps once had a figure in each of its four niches but they vanished long before this photograph was taken. The cross was restored in 1878 and lacks the purity of the one at Aylburton. This used to be the centre of the market, with the old market house near it. The cattle market was held on the first Tuesday of every month, fairs on 4th May and 8th November, and a wool and stock fair on 25th June. Behind the cross is a branch of the Capital and Counties Bank which was later absorbed into Lloyds.

LYDNEY, Newerne Street, C. 1908.

LYDNEY, High Street, early twentieth century. Saddler and harness maker on the left; there were at least two in Lydney in 1901, Thomas Taylor in Newerne Street and Samuel Hewlett Merrick – the name on the sign cannot be seen here, so perhaps this was the latter's shop. There is a barber's shop and tobacconist combined; proprietor William Wood, 1901. In this street at that time were also Benjamin Ensor, shoemaker, and George Phillips, blacksmith.

MINSTERWORTH, date unknown, possibly late 1890s. The cottage has been demolished (note the size of the reap hooks and the woman's hat). In those days women did not want to get sunburned and those who worked in the fields usually wore large bonnets to shield their faces from the sun.

MITCHELDEAN, Mill End, late nineteenth century. Left: distinctive chimney and lamp — Mitcheldean had its own gasworks. The second building on the left is thought to be the old workhouse workshops. In 1835 Mitcheldean became part of Westbury Union with a workhouse at Westbury. Back right: the tall roof of The George can just be seen. To the right of the half-timbered house is the Jovial Collier public house.

MITCHELDEAN with Breakheart Hill behind. The George, that most interesting and impressive building, three storeys high with its tower-like wings, can be seen centre. The brewery is just to our left of it.

MITCHELDEAN. St Michael's Church with its splendid slender spire; timber yard in foreground with wagon, and allotments behind the road. George James Smith owned the steam sawmills (note the chimney). The street is called Mill End.

Market Place. Mitcheldean. Glos

MITCHELDEAN. Market Hall, c. 1909. Built in 1710, it later had its lower parts enclosed. Mitcheldean once had a market on Mondays, and fairs for the sale of horses, cattle, sheep and cheese on Easter Monday and 10th October. The proprietor of the Carisbrooke Temperance Hotel was L.A. Baynham; horses and carriages of every description could be obtained at the shortest notice.

NAILBRIDGE. Left: Speedwell Siding with Trafalgar Colliery coal trucks.

NAILBRIDGE AND HARRY HILL (HARROW), C. 1907. Forest Church, back right; middle, extreme right, is the blacksmith's shop.

NEWLAND, 1909.

NEWNHAM, Britannia Inn, before 1900. Down street is Alfred Barnes, hairdresser; newsagent; and Shortman, clockmaker, whose premises were later occupied by Lloyds Bank.

NEWNHAM, High Street, c. 1909. Obviously it was the children who caught the photographer's eye, just as they now catch ours, but unfortunately one little girl could not keep still for the camera. Boys usually had iron hoops and girls hoops of wood. Second left: Henry Burnett's bakery which sold home-made veal and ham pies, pork pies, game pies, hams, tongues, boar's heads, boned turkey, ices and jellies, as well as bread and cakes, and also provided luncheons and teas.

PARKEND. Left: Old Bear Public House. The signal box is of timber construction. The wheel of the Parkend Colliery Castlemain pumping engine is in the background.

PARKEND. Left: some of the houses known collectively as 'The Square'. These three-storey houses were built in 1851 for the tinplate workers, and are now demolished. Centre: just beyond the motor car, is the Travellers Rest signal box.

RUARDEAN, C. 1908. Photograph taken from the church tower.

RUSPIDGE. Buckshaft Iron Mine was still working and its smoke can be seen (top left). The mine was opened in 1835 and abandoned in 1899.

ST BRIAVELS. At the beginning of the century St Briavels had several shops, including at least three grocers, a shoemaker, saddler, wheelwright, blacksmith and miller.

UPPER SOUDLEY AND BRADLEY HILL. White Horse Inn, centre, and, above and to our left, the chapel. Soudley has a history of iron-making dating back to the thirteenth century.

THE SPEECH HOUSE INN before it was enlarged in 1883. It stands at the traditional centre of the Forest. Built in 1676, as the Lodge in King's Walk, by 1858 it had become an inn although the Verderers still held court there as they still do. Left, back row, in the top hat, is Sir James Campbell, Deputy Surveyor.

THE SPEECH HOUSE, C. 1900. The older part is on the right overlooking the Cannop Valley. The structure, partly of glass, on the roof (left) is something of a mystery. Was it an observatory, a lantern, a folly, or what? I have been unable to discover its purpose or when it disappeared. Surely somebody must know. In the field to the left the Forest of Dean miners used to hold their Annual Demonstration on the second Saturday in July.

STAUNTON. The white house was the Post Office.

STEAM MILLS, 1901. The chimney of Wintle's Steam Flour Mill.

WESTBURY, C. 1900. Left: The Red Lion (formerly The Lion and recorded in 1715), later re-modelled with mock timber framing. Centre: Stone cross, erected to commemorate Queen Victoria's Jubilee in 1887. Right: Westbury Mill. In 1717 Westbury had two corn-mills under one roof. Soon after 1900 the breast-wheel seen here was changed for a turbine. The mill ceased working c. 1928.

WESTBURY. Court and garden, c. 1930. The garden was laid out c. 1700 and this house built in 1885 and demolished in 1961. The stone figure is popularly supposed to be Neptune, but legend has it that he was a river god found in the Severn. Legend also has it that when he heard the church clock strike one a.m. he came down for a bathe. No doubt if he *could* hear the clock he would do so. The position of his right arm suggests a trident but there is not one in the photograph.

WHITECLIFF TURNPIKE (near Coleford), 31 October 1888. This was the last day of the turnpikes, the gates were then thrown open and tolls abolished. 1888, incidentally, was also the year when the poet, F.W. Harvey, was born.

YORKLEY   'This city never found in maps,
              Nor e'en described in gazetteer,
              Is quite as singular, perhaps,
              As any city, far or near.

From *Yorkley City*, by Richard Morse, 1840

Really a large and scattered hamlet, which has given its name to a coal seam, and was once mostly a community of colliers.

Collieries and Colliers

'The Forest of Dean is full of coal'
                              John Byng 1781

FREE MINERS' LEVEL near Blakeney, 1901. Forest coal mining as it *was* before the big collieries opened and as it *is* now they have closed.

CANNOP COLLIERY, sunk 1906. Ceased working 27 August 1960.

CRUMP MEADOW COLLIERY, sunk 1824. Ceased working 17 July 1929. Front left: engine house with rope to headgear. Background right: Foxes Bridge Colliery. Background centre: Foxes Bridge spoil heap.

EASTERN UNITED COLLIERY, c. 1913. Sunk 1909 and abandoned 30 January 1959. This was a large drift mine. Above it was the older Walmore into which Eastern cut. The spoil at the time was tipped on the other side of road (right), close to Shakemantle Iron Mine.

FLOUR MILL COLLIERY. First galed 1843 and sunk 1872. Passed to the owners of Princess Royal 1886. The Flour Mill and Park Gutter were connected underground in 1916 and kept open for Princess Royal. Coal was still being brought up Flour Mill shafts in 1928. Closed in 1931, but a small staff was still working there later (see next photograph).

JOVIAL FORESTERS whose trade was getting coal. Colliers at the Flour Mill in the 1940s. Note the caps and scarves, hobnailed boots and moleskin trousers – with yorks tied just below the knees on the third man in the front row. Also the Tommy bag for food and can for water or cold tea. Carbide lamps (naked lights) were used in the Forest. In the front row, far right, is William Nash. The colliers wore skullcaps while working and stripped to singlet, trousers and boots.

FOXES BRIDGE COLLIERY, sunk 1855–60. Ceased working 10 August 1930. Trucks can be seen under the screen (centre); full trucks in the foreground. 126,978 tons of coal was raised in 1880.

LIGHTMOOR COLLIERY, c. 1910. Sunk 1830 and ceased working 15 June 1940. Top left is the arm of a beam-pump. In the background the North pit is on the left and the South pit on the right, together with production shafts and headframes. Shaft left, foreground; beam-pump brought water up this shaft ninety yards and then the water ran down Mere Brook Level and entered brook at Ruspidge. The mouth of Mere Brook Level can be seen by the football ground. The engine house is still standing, the only one left in the whole of the Forest.

COLLIERS AT MEADOWCLIFF COLLIERY. This colliery was started by a Mr Cowmeadow and a Mr Ratcliffe.

NORCHARD COLLIERS AT THE SIDINGS. Norchard sidings opened 1906 and closed 31 December 1960. The original siding that served Norchard was known as Kidnalls Siding. In 1923, the West Gloucestershire Power Station was opened on an adjacent site. The power station closed in 1957, and Norchard closed too. Far right: D. Virgo, the foreman.

PATCHES PIT, Christchurch, *c.* 1930. Fred Jones and Tom Hughes are on the photograph. Note the peculiar structure of the head-frame.

PRINCESS ROYAL COLLIERY. Galed in 1842 to Priest Brothers, all four of them free miners, but afterwards it changed hands several times. Abandoned 1963.

SEAM AT PRINCESS ROYAL. 1 September 1927. A heading – roadway to a seam – and steel arches instead of the more usual timbers used. Timber props are supporting the ripping – the amount of rock etc. to be removed in order to fit steel arches. Typical Forest-type tub, truck, tram or dram.

PROSPER PIT, near Coalway. One of the last two wooden headframes in the Forest; Ellwood was the other one.

STRIP-AND-AT-IT COLLIERY, BRIERLEY, c. 1900. Working in the mid-nineteenth century, later it became part of Trafalgar. Typical outlay of old Forest, house-coal collieries – full trucks to screens and empties away by gravity.

FLOODING AT UNION PIT; the rescued and the rescuers. (Note, water can and tommy bag slung over shoulders of man on left). At midday on Thursday, 4 September 1902, water from an old working broke into the Union Coal Pit at Bix Head Slade Bottom. The water flooded the pit, sweeping away timbers and trapping several colliers. Four men lost their lives: William Martin, aged 30, married with four children; Thomas James, aged 28, married with one child; his brother Amos, aged 20; Hubert Gwatkins, aged 26, whose body was not found for ten days. Their funerals were attended by Sir Charles and Lady Dilke who were staying at the Speech House at the time of the disaster. Two colliers were trapped in the pit for one hundred and twenty hours before being rescued.

TRAFALGAR COLLIERY. Closed 1925. It had two shafts very close together – as can be seen, right – they were the closest in the Forest. Trafalgar was the first mine in the world to use electric power (1883). Also the first to use electric detonators. The first pit strike to occur in the Forest was at Trafalgar in July 1871.

CAGE ABOUT TO DESCEND TO TRAFALGAR. A cage with a safety gate. At the end of the shift a man wearing a harness went down on top of the cage to inspect the lining of the shaft.

WATERLOO COLLIERY (also known as Arthur and Edward), sunk 1860. Ceased working 23 December 1959. Typical outlay. Shaft only 90 yards deep. Note that there are no screens – full tubs went up an incline (approximately a half to one mile long) crossing over the Coleford–Gloucester road to screens on the other side – the famous 'Creeper'.

RESCUE PARTY. Water broke into Waterloo from the old East Slade Pit on 30 June 1949. Five men were trapped, fortunately one of them, Oswald Simmons, knew a way through old workings to the disued New Pit at the Pludds. A few hours after the flooding they were all brought to safety through this disused shaft.

THE WINNER PIT. Engine house and tramway. The shale is being taken to the Broadmoor Brick Works. This was one of the highest production, small-housecoal pits in Dean.

FOUR COLLIERS, C. 1922: Cyril Davies, Fred Davies, Moses Edwards, and Hubert Edwards. Their attire is typical; the caps, moleskin trousers with yorks, the boots, and the carbide pit lamps. Many colliers walked through the woods and over the hills to work; in the dark with their lamps shining, the procession looked like a string of pearls. These four are between Knockley Wood and Parkend. They are going or coming from work, either from Castlemain or from Parkend to the Flour Mill or to Park Gutter, or vice versa.

FOREST OF DEAN MINERS ASSOCIATION; date, location, band, and people unknown, despite many enquiries. The inn sign cannot be seen, only the licencee's name – Ernest Stanley. 'Lodge No. 12 is on the banner. It could be Lane End, Coalway, or perhaps Viney Hill. Note the roof, with two courses of stone, then slate. A miners' union in the form of 'a union club' was first formed in the Forest in 1871, and later became a branch of the Amalgamated Association of Miners with eighteen lodges and a membership of four-and-a-half thousand. Timothy Mountjoy was the first Miners' Agent in the Forest. The A.A.M. collapsed in 1874, the Miners' Union in the Forest weakened and suffered defeats and was disbanded. Mountjoy was discharged in 1877 and a new District Union was formed in 1882.

MINERS HOLDING A MEETING in woods near Speech House during the 1926 strike. There were riots in Cinderford. Miners had to get vouchers in order to get basic food such as bread, and some families were turned away.

LAST DAY AT PRINCESS ROYAL COLLIERY, 1963. This was the last shift and the last of Princess Royal. An old collier who had worked in Princess Royal to the end told me that there are thousands of tons of coal still there.

END OF THE ERA, 1965. One of the very last trucks of coal from Northern United Colliery. In the photograph taken by Alex Pope, is Bert Hyett. Seven hundred men had been employed. This and the preceding photograph are outside the period of this book, but both really belong to it, in that they signify the real end of an important and character-making epoch of Forest history. Northern United, sunk 1933, was the last of the big collieries in Dean to be opened and the last to be worked, it was abandoned 25 December 1965. Its closure meant the end of a way of life in the Forest.

The Severn Shore

'My lovely Severn shines as bright
As any moon on trucks of coal,
Or sun above our greenest meadows'

W.H. Davies

OVER BRIDGE, C. 1902. The bridge that led the way to the Forest. Built by Thomas Telford (1826–29), the span of the arch exceeded any other in the Kingdom at the time.

BERT GREENING WITH A PORPOISE caught at Minsterworth C. 1940. A school of dolphin came up the river in the late 1930s – forty-seven were counted at Minsterworth. Porpoise often come up the river; a small whale reached Awre in July 1943. All of these species are mammals and must have air; their tails move up and down, not side to side and they must have a depth of water. Consequently they perish in the Severn at low tide.

SALMON FISHING AT PLACKETPOOL, Minsterworth. Bert Greening in the boat, George Bennett and Bill Greening. Note the puntlike boat and flake (the wood staging behind the net on the shore). A winch is also used in these higher fishing places – but downstream at Framilode, Elton Meadow, Broadoak, etc. neither flake nor winch is used because of the advantage of a good stretch of sand. On the Severn the season for salmon fishing by long-nets is 2nd February to 31st July with a weekly closed time from 12 mid-day Saturday to 6 a.m. Monday. The long-net may be up to two hundred yards in length. A crew of four men is needed, two on the boat – paying out net – and two on the banks or shore.

THE SEVERN FROZEN AT MINSTERWORTH (church on the left), January 1940.

ELVER FISHING. The same stretch of the Severn as before, spring 1940.

OUTSIDE THE SLOOP, the riverside inn at Bollow, 23 October 1904. (Photographed by Jim Gleed). Formerly the Bollow House Inn, it closed during the 1920s.

GARDEN CLIFF. At the Cleeve, Westbury, seventy feet above the Severn. It shows a section of Rhaetic beds. Peat and forest-bed fossil remains have been found and a large bone – by tradition the thigh bone of a giant. Fools' gold, iron pyrites is found here. Garden is a corruption of 'Garne', the mediaeval name for this part of the parish. About two hundred yards downstream, is Severn Mill fed directly by the stream. Its proximity to the riverbank has led some people to suppose that it was a tide-mill. The cattle in this photograph are the once popular Shorthorns.

SALMON FISHING AT BROADOAK, 1930s. Just landing and it looks as if there are two or three fish in the net.

THE FROZEN SEVERN AT NEWNHAM, February 1917. The warehouse can be seen on the left. The quay and warehouse at Newnham Pill were built and owned by Hawkin, Pyrke and Company during the latter half of the eighteenth century. Robert Pyrke was an attorney at Newnham in 1759; he and Thomas Hawkin were co-owners of *The Severn*, a brig of one hundred and eight tons which traded to London 1764–80.

SEVERN STREET (formerly Passage), Newnham, early twentieth century. To me a most romantic sight, this steep, narrow street with the broad expanse of the Severn below. Top left: The Upper George, one of Newnham's oldest buildings and containing the Sanctuary Room – once a detached part of the Hundred of St Briavels. Bottom right: on the corner, the former Bear, an old coaching inn. John Byng, the traveller and diarist, stopped here in June 1781: 'I entered the Bear Inn at Newnham, with a good appetite, and found a round of beef just taken from the pot, which I strove to devour, and likewise a gooseberry pie.'

THE FERRY AT NEWNHAM. The horse-boat left. The ferry was recorded in 1457 and closed in 1948. In his *Journals*, George Sturt states that as many as four hundred Welsh cattle had been seen waiting here to be taken across the river in the nineteenth century.

NEWNHAM FERRY FROM ARLINGHAM, c. 1908. Warehouse far right. In those days Arlingham was Newnham's neighbour and Mr Hirom who had a bakery on the Green went over on the ferry regularly to sell bread and cakes at Arlingham.

THE SEASIDE OF THE FOREST — on the sands at Newnham, 1920s. The warehouse, which had become the Drill Hall, is on the left. From Cinderford and Littledean they walked to spend a Saturday or Sunday afternoon on the sands. When the rail-motor service started in 1907 the Cinderford people came by rail. Afterwards they had tea at Carefield's restaurant, or Burnett's in the High Street; or up the steps in the photograph we saw of Severn Street and into the Upper George's Tearoom.

LOADING COAL INTO THE *FINIS*, Bullo Dock, 1920s. This barge used to take coal to Gloucester, to Brimscombe and to Frampton, it also carried stone. Bullo Pill Dock was opened between 1810–20. The tramway from the Forest came under the Haie Hill, through the world's first railway tunnel (1809). Bullo Dock ceased to work in 1926 and the *Finis* was the last boat to use it officially. The remains of the *Finis* now lie under the pill-box (built in 1940) on the Arlingham Bank.

SALMON FISHING WITH A LONG-NET at Box Hole, Bullo, 1927. William Trigg and his son Edgar. Note the different type of boat from the one at Placketpool. This boat had been the tow-boat belonging to the *Finis*.

TWO MEN AND A BOAT, Awre. Walter Cadogan and Henry Cadogan. There have been Cadogans at Awre for three hundred years, for generations they have been salmon fishers, and there are still Cadogans fishing for salmon at Awre today.

PUTCHON WEIR for catching salmon at Woodend, Awre. A photograph taken in 1914 by Fred Blanton of Newnham. The season for catching salmon by putcheons starts 16th April and ends 15th August with no weekly closed time. The mouths of the putcheons face the out-flowing tide and can only catch salmon swimming downstream. Fishermen have to work with the tide, and the salmon must be removed before the incoming tide washes them out of the putcheons, or before birds or even foxes can reach them. The putcheons also have to be cleared of seaweed and debris which would otherwise block them. At the end of the season the putcheons are removed. The frame of the weir, which was made of elm posts with larch cross-bars, remained.

FRANK CADOGAN (son of Walter) with lave-net and salmon, 1920s. Lave-net fishing has the same season and weekly closed periods as long-net fishing. Lave-nets can only be used at low tide because the fishermen have to wade into the water. Fishermen make their own nets; the rimes (arms) are made of hazel or sallow, the staff of ash or birch. Some fishermen prefer to wear shorts and go barefoot into the river, the immediate contact with the sand enables them to know whether it is firm or quick.

LAVE-NET FISHERMAN AT AWRE, 1920s. An extended lave-net in the boat and a lot of salmon in the foreground.

THREE MEN IN A BOAT, Awre 1920s. When the lave-net fishermen reach their fishing ground, the boat is anchored and they wade into the water. On reaching their chosen places, their nets are spread out and they watch the water keenly. They look for the mark of the salmon, which is a long white line. The salmon can swim faster than the fisherman can run. The fisherman's advantage lies with his being 'on home ground'. By knowing the effects of wind and tide on the river bed, he can tell what the salmon will do. He must get in front to 'make his lave'.

COLIN AND WALTER CADOGAN, sons of Frank Cadogan, with lave-nets and putcheons at Woodend, Awre c. 1950. Both were also farmers, and Colin Cadogan a grower of and dealer in cider fruit.

WALTER CADOGAN MAKING PUTCHEONS at Woodend, c. 1950. The putcheons are made of withy, though the staves may be of hazel. The Cadogans had their own withy beds. Note the fruit pullar (basket), also made of withy, by the stove; and the boat, which will receive attention during the closed season.

GATCOMBE AT HIGH WATER, C. 1920. Stopper boats to the left of the house. Gatcombe was again under water like this on 13 December 1982.

LAVE-NET FISHERMEN at Well House Bay, 1930s. Part of the Severn Railway Bridge can be seen on the right.

STOPPER BOAT FISHING AT GATCOMBE. Searching for the salmon. This type of fishing has the same season and weekly closed periods as the long-net and lave-net fishing. Stop boats fish on flood and ebb tides, and so catch in-coming and out-going salmon. The boats fish on wires – a wire rope fixed to the shore and to a mooring in the river. The net is spread out on rimes from the boat and passes beneath it, the force of the river current forming it into a bag. The rimes are dipped into the water and held up by a prop. The fisherman holds strings attached to various parts of the net, when he feels the pull of a fish, the prop is kicked out and the fish is caught.

FISHERMEN AT GATCOMBE, c. 1922. Then there were ten stop-boats, now there are only three; seventy-eight men fished with lave-nets, now only four.

END OF SEASON AT GATCOMBE, 1932. Stop-boat being pulled in on rollers at Court House, which was bought by the Morse family in 1878. Then the boats were owned by Christopher Morse, today the family tradition is carried on by his son-in-law Raymond Bayliss and by Mrs Anne Bayliss who makes the nets, and the boats are brought in by tractor.

PART OF LYDNEY DOCK as it was eighty or more years ago. Entrance to Pidcock's Canal. The building in the background is the Severn and Wye Railway and Canal Company's original office (1813). Pidcock's Canal went up to the iron-works.

LYDNEY DOCK. The harbour was officially opened in 1813. Note the coal shutes on the left. Coal was shipped to Bridgewater, Bristol, Channel Isles, Combe Martin, Ilfracombe, Minehead, and the Scillies.

SECTION FOUR

Wyeside

'O Sylvan Wye! thou wanderer through the woods,
How often has my spirit turned to thee!'
William Wordsworth

THE WYE AT LYDBROOK. Centre: a travelling fair; the roundabout can be seen, and also traction engines taking water at the riverside. The Lydbrook viaduct is on the right.

THE WYE AND RAILWAY AT SYMOND'S YAT, C. 1912. The Ross–Monmouth Railway opened 4 August 1873; the passenger service closed in 1959 and freight in 1964.

RAILWAY STATION AT SYMOND'S YAT, C. 1905. The railway tunnel, four hundred and ninety-five yards in length, went under the Yat Rock.

SYMOND'S YAT and the 'wanderer through the woods'.

FERRY AT SYMOND'S YAT.

REDBROOK, railway and bridge. The Monmouth to Chepstow line opened in 1876, the passenger service closed in 1959, and freight in 1964.

REDBROOK. It once had two breweries, both demolished c. 1950. There were also two copper works, which became tinplate works in the eighteenth century, with warehouses and a wharf at the river. Redbrook's tinplate was exported all over the world. The works finally closed in 1961.

REDBROOK, showing the railway station, left.

BIGSWEIR BRIDGE. A cast-iron arch, build 1825–8 when a new turnpike road to Chepstow was constructed. Left: the toll house. Bigsweir Railway Station (Monmouth/Chepstow line) was renamed St Briavels Station in 1927.

BROCKWEIR VILLAGE, c. 1905. 'Brock-Wear, which may be deemed the Fourth Port on the Wye.' – Charles Heath, early nineteenth century. In 1820, Brockweir had sixteen public houses. A halt was added to the Monmouth–Chepstow railway line at Brockweir in 1929. On one day John Parry of Brockweir caught one hundred and fifteen salmon.

BROCKWEIR BEFORE THE BRIDGE. A ferry was in operation, the crossing cost one penny – c. 1900. Centre: sixteenth-century Manor House. Kelp (seaweed) for fertiliser was one of Brockweir's imports.

BRIDGE AT BROCKWEIR. The bridge was built in 1904.

TROWS AT BROCKWEIR. Trows were built here, and a number of them traded to ports in the Bristol Channel. Among them was the *William and Sarah*.

BEACHLEY, launching of the *War Glory*, 1920. National shipyards were constructed at Beachley and Chepstow in 1917, at a cost of six million pounds, and incorporating thirty slipways. However, the war ended before a ship was launched, but eventually the *War Glory* was launched into the Wye.

Mainly Agriculture

'Agriculture is, or should be the greatest of the crafts'
Lord Northbourne

PLOUGHING AT LONGCROFT FARM, WESTBURY, 1926. (D. Larner and J. Bullock). Two horses were usually used, especially on easy, worked land such as this. A young horse was sometimes put between two older horses in order to train it, but these are all mature horses and I am unable to explain why three are being used, unless the field was being ploughed extra deeply.

AT WYNCOLLS FARM, ELTON, May 1918. At this time, with the menace of U-Boats to our shipping and food supplies, England wanted every bit of corn that English farms could grow. As in this instance, the authorities sent men and horses to speed the ploughing-up of grassland in order to grow more corn. The soldier's name was Haycock. The two young ladies looking on are the farmer's daughters – the Misses E. and B. Hague.

EXAMINING HORSES FOR THE ARMY, First World War. The authorities commandeered horses, which partly explains the previous photograph as well.

'AND THE MOWER WHETS THE SCYTHE', 1901. Note the length of the blade and the belt around the corduroy trousers in which the mower carried his sharpening stone. A good man could mow an acre of grass in a day, and it would be a good man who could swing this scythe. The tool, so apparently clumsy, in the hands of a skilled man became a thing of grace and beauty.

'O sound to rout the brood of cares,
The sweep of scythe in morning dew.'

MOWING GRASS AT COLLIER'S BEECH, NEAR BREAM, 1930s. Fred Morgan on the mowing machine. Mowing was gruelling work for horses. The first horse-drawn mowers appearing in the late 1850s.

TURNING HAY AT COURT FARM, MITCHELDEAN, 1920s. Albert Phelps on the swath-turner. Horse drawn swath-turners first appeared in the 1880s, and the type shown here was in general use until the 1950s.

HAYMAKING AT HART'S BARN, LONGHOPE, 1935. Mr Jobling, Gordon Few, Ernie Martin, and Wally Parkes, at the back, Clary Taylor. A pause for a drink of cider.

'Oh, let the cider flow
In ploughing and in sowing –
The healthiest drink I know,
In reaping and in mowing.'

HAYMAKERS AT LYDNEY off to get another load. This could have been in the 1920s or 1950s, but was probably taken in the '40s. The number of men would be reduced to two today.

AN OLD-FASHIONED KNACKER'S CART near Blakeney. There does not seem room, but a dead horse would be carried in this cart. The tail-board is partly obscured by the second horse.

DIPPING SHEEP AT BRIERLEY, 1930s. Moses Baldwin with his sons, Aaron and Harry.

TIBBS CROSS, near Littledean, Autumn, 1956. That Autumn there was an outbreak of foot and mouth disease in the Forest, and these sheep have been rounded up for slaughter and were buried in an adjacent small field. For some time afterwards the Forest was devoid of its roaming sheep. Note the policeman at the road junction. Many Foresters will recognise the markings on the ewes.

JAMES PHELPS OF COURT FARM, MITCHELDEAN with dog and sheep, 1930. This was my grandfather who loved sheep; he lived for ninety-two years and kept sheep for eighty-seven of those years.

JAMES GREEN OF FLAXLEY with Shorthorn cow, three-legged milking stool and pail, 1930. The cow was obviously a personal friend.

MILKING COMPETITION AT GRANGE COURT, March 1943. Hand-milking was still general practice. Some of the young ladies were farmers' daughters, others were members of the Women's Land Army, and some are now farmers' wives.

FRUIT PICKERS AT DENE RISE, BLAKENEY, c. 1924.

GEESE AT BRAINS GREEN, 1901.

'The fault is great in man or woman
Who steals a goose from off the common;
But what can plead that man's excuse
Who steals a common from a goose?'

TURKEYS AT BOSELEY, C. 1920. The turkeys are a breed called Bronze which is now extremely rare. Right: Arthur Ebborn and Miss Betty Ebborn. The building in the background has a cider mill.

DUCKS AT HOWBEACH, 1901

'From troubles of the world
I turn to ducks,
Beautiful comical things.'
F.W. Harvey.

POULTRY AT MONK HILL, FLAXLEY, early 1930s. Some of the King family with ducks, geese, hens and a guinea fowl in the foreground.

PIGS AT LONGHOPE, 1937. Oliver Halford is the pigman.

HARVEST AT NORTHWOOD. Oats being cut and stooked. The sails of the reaper/binder can be seen behind the horses. The boys have probably been catching rabbits as they run out of the standing corn. Oats were left in stooks until the church bells had rung for three consecutive Sundays.

CIDERMAKING AT EDGE HILLS. Apples were put in the circular trough and crushed by the stone wheel; the crushed apples were then placed in a press and the juice extracted, then poured into barrels to 'work' and mature. The wheel is of course made of Forest stone. The hard-wearing Forest Stone (conglomerate) was resistant to the acid of the fruit, and was used extensively elsewhere. The circular stone troughs and runner-stone (propelled by a horse) were fashioned at the quarries.

Other Work and Workers

'Man goeth forth to his work, and to his labour . . .'
Psalms

PARKEND FURNACES, 1908. The chimney seen being demolished was for the boilers of the blast or blowing engine. The building on the right (which still stands) was the engine house which later housed the Forestry School. The furnaces were demolished in 1890.

THE MALTINGS AND TRANSPORT, Forest Brewery, Mitcheldean, c. 1922. Known variously as the Forest Steam Brewery, the Mitcheldean, or Wintle's Brewery. The buildings are of sandstone blocks from the Wilderness Quarry and were erected in 1868, the Maltings in 1872. The Brewery's slogan was: 'Mitcheldean Ales – Best in the West'. More than one-hundred-and-seventy licensed premises were supplied; not only in the Forest (which accounted for about eighty-three), but as far away as Abergavenny, Crickhowell, Gloucester, Hereford, Monmouth, Pontypool, as well as Ross, Tintern, Usk and other places. Those who can remember drinking Mitcheldean beer say it was the best they have ever drunk. The Brewery and its products were extolled by the Brewers' Journal in 1923 and yet within a short time the Brewery closed.

WORKERS AT STONE WORKS, Parkend.

QUARRY AT THE PLUMP, ABENHALL, 1 September 1894. Four tons of powder fired at one blast in a small tunnel driven into the rock by Aaron Simmonds.

FOX'S CARPENTER'S SHOP, near Seven Stars, Cinderford, c. 1900.

WORKERS AT FRED WATKINS ENGINEERING, Sling, 1942.

TIN WORKS, Lydney, 1905. That tall chimney (right) was more than one-hundred-and-sixty feet high. This large works closed in 1957. In 1905 it had about five hundred workers.

CEMENT WORKS, Mitcheldean, 1907. Started c. 1894; closed c. 1919. Shortly after this photograph was taken the works employed about two hundred men and produced more than fifty tons of cement each day. In this photograph the works has some female visitors (centre).

WORKERS AT THE WAGON WORKS, Bullo Pill, c. 1900. The foreman can be recognised by his bowler hat, the usual attire of foremen. Note the broad gauge line. The works were variously known as Bullo Pill Wagon Works, and Standard Wagon Works Co. Ltd. Owned by Joseph Boucher in 1870, they were taken over by Forest of Dean Wagon Co. in 1890. Railway stock was built and repaired, also wheels. I have been told that a railway buffer, which was in universal use and known as Boucher's Buffer, was invented here. The works must have closed shortly after this photograph was taken and later the site was occupied by a Rubber Mill.

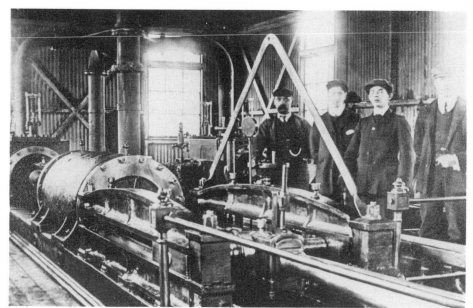

COMPRESSOR AND ATTENDANTS. New Fancy Colliery, c. 1905.

TIMBER FELLERS, near Longhope, c. 1909. Standing on the tree trunk: William Bowkett. Sitting by him and wearing a waistcoat: Charles Bowkett. The young lady in white has probably brought the men some food and drink. Surprisingly, five of the men have removed their waistcoats. All appear to be wearing yorks, belts and braces; two have kerchiefs. Note that the tree has been felled in leaf; also the long, shaped cross-cut saw, and large English pattern felling axes.

TIMBER FELLERS, Chestnut Wood, Popes Hill, July 1941. In the group are Cyril, Frank, Sydney and Fred (Skipper) Jones. This would have been at the time of a large scale felling of Chestnut trees.

GEORGE NELMES, BEEKEEPER, Pembroke Street, Cinderford, c. 1901. Note the different styles of beehives.

HARVESTING POTATOES ON ALLOTMENTS. Lydney, First World War. Springfields Chapel in the background.

OPENING OF DILKE MEMORIAL HOSPITAL, Lightmoor, Cinderford, 1923. Back row, far right: M.L. Bangara, M.B. Ch.B. D.Ph. Front, second Left: G.H. Rowlinson. Also W. Meredith, Dr. Beadle, Dr. Rigden. The hospital was built in 1922.

WHITECROFT PIN WORKS, May 1949. Pin-making was an old Forest industry and its pins went to most parts of the world.

Open for Business

'The professed shopkeeper has generally a taint of the artist somewhere about him'
Samuel Butler

INDIA AND CHINA TEA CO., PROVISIONS AND GROCERIES, CINDERFORD *c.* 1910. Home-cured bacon, 9*d.* per lb; tea 1/8*d* and 1/4*d* – but remember the wages of the time, and that a great many people could not afford these prices.

PONT AND ADAMS, ST JOHN'S STREET, COLEFORD, *c.* 1909. Their cake was 4*d*, 6*d* and 8*d* per lb; the bacon home-cured. In this and other photographs of shops, note the larger number of goods on display and the artistry with which they are displayed.

J. KEAR AND SONS, THE TRIANGLE, CINDERFORD. These premises were later occupied by George Whittle, grocer, and now Bowers, chemist, is on this site.

OWEN STALEY, HIGH STREET, MITCHELDEAN. Owen Staley and District Nurse Bailey are on the right. He was grocer, corn, meal and flour merchant, ham and bacon curer, general draper, milliner, boot and shoe factor, outfitter and General supplier. All the buildings in the scene have been demolished except the building which housed Owen Staley's business.

ALBERT PRICE, BUTCHER, NEWNHAM, c. 1906. The man outside the shop is unknown. Some good hoggets on the railings, but such a display would not be allowed today. All meat sold here was produced locally. Once a coaching inn known as the Lamb and Flag.

J.H. PARRY, GREENGROCER, HIGH STREET, CINDERFORD, early 1920s. Established in 1881 and still in business. The round fruit pots and rectangular baskets were probably made at Severnside. Note the roundabout, back right.

F.R. BOWER, CHEMIST AND STATIONER, 1910. Note the news placards – 'Dr Crippen Defence.' Crippen was tried at the Old Bailey for the murder of his wife and executed at Pentonville 23 November 1910.

E.G. ANNETTS, PRACTICAL WATCHMAKER AND JEWELLER, High Street, Cinderford c. 1909. This shop also sold 'burglar alarms (properly fitted) genuine Edison phonographs, electrical pocket lamps and electric clocks that never want winding.'

WILLIAMS BROS., VICTORIA STREET, CINDERFORD, c. 1909. This and other photographs show how local shops supplied almost every possible type of goods. Living in the Forest was not as remote as some reminiscences would have you believe. Cinderford, for example, was town; there was little need to travel further afield.

C.B. SMALE, NEWERNE STREET, LYDNEY, 1910. Another example of a local shop supplying a great variety of household needs.

TROTTER, MARKET PLACE, COLEFORD, c. 1909.

PROVIS AND HORWOOD, MARKET PLACE, COLEFORD, c. 1909. Drapers, silk mercers, milliners, ladies outfitters; carpets, rugs, floor cloths.

STANLEY WILCE, HIGH STREET, CINDERFORD, c. 1910. Stanley Wilce in doorway.

G.B. KILMINSTER, BOOT DEALER, ST JOHN'S STREET, COLEFORD, c. 1909. 'Quality high, prices low.'

TERRETT TAYLOR & SONS, COLEFORD, C. 1909. General ironmongers, house furnishers; also agents for agricultural implements, builders, timber and slate merchants.

STINCHCOMBE, HIGH STREET, MITCHELDEAN, C. 1901. This shop, miraculously, still stands. I say 'miraculously' because it seems the only explanation for its survival or for that of any other old buildings in Mitcheldean – a town which has suffered the full wrath and vigour of 'the improvers'. At the time of writing this, yet another old building, the former Red Lion, has fallen victim.

School, Religion, Music

'It really is of importance, not only what men do, but also what manner of men they are that do it. Among the works of man, which human life is rightly employed in perfecting and beautifying, the first in importance is surely man himself'

J.S. Mill

MINSTERWORTH SCHOOL, c. 1900.

DOUBLE VIEW SCHOOL, CINDERFORD, c. 1908. Group 10. J.A. Emery, headmaster, of whom Leonard Clark wrote in *A Fool in the Forest*.

STEAM MILLS SCHOOL, c. 1900.

BLAISDON SCHOOL, 1912.

THE SCOWLES SCHOOL, NEAR COLEFORD, c. 1914.

SOUDLEY SCHOOL. Group 1, c. 1924. Headmaster: A. Hull.

ELLWOOD SCHOOL, 1928. Master (left): H.R. Harvey. Headmaster (right): B. Kear.

MITCHELDEAN SCHOOL. Group 2, 1935.

CRAFT SCHOOL, LYDNEY, 1935.

RUARDEAN HILL BAPTIST SUNDAY SCHOOL, c. 1910.

COLEFORD BAPTIST OUTING CLUB, 14 July 1910. Seated right of centre: Rev. A.H. Horlick. There were Baptists in Coleford in the latter part of the 17th century.

YOUNG PEOPLE'S CHRISTIAN ENDEAVOUR — Bream Bible Christian Chapel, 1898. (Now under the heading of Parkend Road Methodist Church, Bream). The chapel was built in 1851.

DRYBROOK CONGREGATIONAL LADIES CHOIR, c. 1948. Congregationalists, formerly Independents, were the leading Nonconformist denomination in the Forest during the early nineteenth century. Their pleasant, square, simple chapels can be seen at several places in the Forest including Mitcheldean, Littledean, Blakeney and Coleford.

WESTBURY ON SEVERN CHURCH CHOIR, c. 1913. The group includes: back, not in surplices, bell ringers T. Hart, A. Ayland (carrier), J. Belcher, W. Gleed (smallholder), C. Everness (farmworker); back, in surplices, A. Gibson, G. Draper (railwayman), J. Hague (farmer), J. Gibson, (coachman), W. Bennett (farmer), A. French (shoemaker), J. Ambrose (wheelwright); middle, seated, W. Gibson, J. Grindon (miller), Rev. Arthur McNamara, (curate, later vicar of Flaxley), C. Cook, (headmaster, Westbury School), A. Ayland.

WHITECROFT MALE VOICE CHOIR, C. 1930. The choir did have as many as a hundred voices, and broadcast several times. It was one of the best choirs in the West of England. Seated behind the cup is Charles Phipps, conductor, with Arthur James (pianist) on his left and Clifton Aldridge, who was secretary/manager of Lydney District Farmers, Ltd., on his right.

BREAM SILVER PRIZE BAND, C. 1928. The shield had just been won at Cheltenham. Evan Jones with medals and baton. Standing on the right, middle row, (not in uniform) is Victor Shingles, who received a certificate in 1973 for fifty years service with the band.

DRYBROOK AND DISTRICT SILVER PRIZE BAND, 1949. Daily Herald Shield (Area Champion) 1949; Ruardean Challenge Cup 1946, 1947, 1948, 1949; Wessex and Gloucestershire Association Champion 1949.

LYDNEY TOWN BAND, November 1901.

Sport, Processions, Occasions

'All sorts and conditions of men'
Book of Common Prayer

FOUNDER MEMBERS OF LYDNEY AND AYLBURTON RFC.
1887 – 88 – 1937 – 38
Jubilee Dinner, Feathers Hotel, Lydney, November 4th, 1937

W. H. Imm, W. Tovey, A. Tawney, C. Howells, C. Kerwood, G. Powell.
W. Probert, The Viscount Bledisloe, William Jones.

FOUNDER MEMBERS OF LYDNEY AND AYLBURTON RUGBY FOOTBALL CLUB. Jubilee Dinner, 1937.

LYDNEY RUGBY FOOTBALL CLUB

Season 1929 – 1930

Undefeated at home.

Last Match—Gloucester v. Lydney, April 22nd.   Result: Lydney 12 pts.; Gloucester 9 pts.

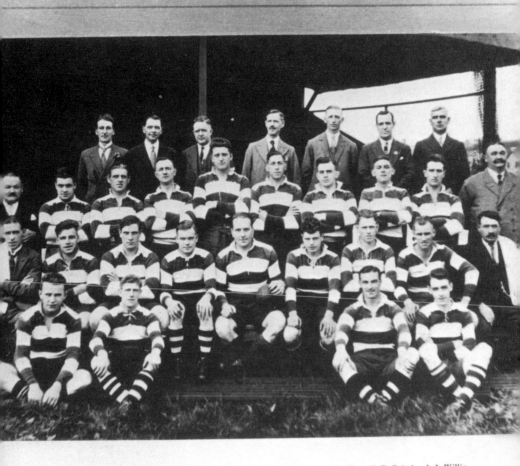

A. Sandford, F. Fletcher, PC Morris, PC Anderson, S. Nelmes, L. Howell, E. Pritchard, J. Willis.
J. Brown, C. Price, W. Probert, PC Taylor (Capt.), R. Moore, J. Jay, W. Thomas.
H. Gardiner, T. Wellington, E. Kelsey, C. Williams.

LYDNEY RUGBY FOOTBALL CLUB, 1929–30. Undefeated at home.

BREAM RUGBY FOOTBALL CLUB, 1921–22. In 1923–24 season Bream played 32, won 22, drew 5, lost 5. Points for, 306; against, 97. Left to right, back row: G. Davis, T. Preest, G. Hughes, T. Stone, J. Worgan, S. Ward, B. James, R. Worgan, R. Preest, S. Birt, A. Jones, C. Cooper. Second row: C. Baker, F. York, J. Wasley, S. Stone, W. Robins (capt), G. Hancocks, F. Moore, W. Dunn, J. Kent. Front row: Kidey Jenkins, A. Vaughan, R. Meek, J. Hall.

CINDERFORD RUGBY FOOTBALL CLUB, 1896–7, with the Bathurst Cup (the original County Cup). Won three years in succession, it then belonged to the Club. Back row: T. Williams, L. Berrows, G. Berrows, W.M. Leighton, W.M. Martin, S. Body. Middle row: A. Mudway, A. Robbins, W.M. Bevan, H.Y. Williams (capt), N. Baldwin, J. Jones. Front row: T. Martin, F. Martin, G. Barbin. The Club was founded in 1892.

MINSTERWORTH ASSOCIATION FOOTBALL CLUB, 1910. Captain, F.W. Harvey was later to become known as the poet of Gloucestershire.

MITCHELDEAN A.F.C., 1912–13.

PARKEND A.F.C., 1923–24. Back left to front right: W. Turley, G. Turley, W. Davies, B. Meredith, H. Morrison, A. Wright; J. Blewitt, J. Roper, B. Adams, J. Mailer, P. Edmunds; W. Richards, J. Williams, W. Davidson, G. Burrows, C. Wellington; A. Parry, T.H. Morgan, C. Morgan, H. Combs, J. Turley.

RUSPIDGE UNITED, 1951–2. North Gloucestershire League Division V. Played 22, won 22. Back row: T. Phelps, – Adams, F. Turley, N. Butt, H. Clarke, D. Holder. Front row: N. Beech, B. Pritchard, A. Treasure, R. Pritchard, K. Holder.

BLAISDON CRICKET CLUB, 1908. The group includes D. Parslow, J. Stephens, D. Preston, P. Woodman (back row), J.S. Bate, F. Parslow, W. Ingham (front).

CINDERFORD RED ROSE CRICKET CLUB, 1910.

FLAXLEY CRICKET CLUB, 1936 – the year Flaxley won the District Cup. The group includes C.H. Bullett, J. Keyse, W.C. Cullen, F. Phelps, G. Keyse, H. Harvey, Mrs H. Young, Marjorie Bullett, S. Vaile, F. Boughton (capt), F. Terry, J. Keyse, Marjorie Boughton, Audrey Boughton, T. Bullett. (Photograph by Fred Blanton).

RECRUITING AT COLEFORD, First World War.

EX-PUPILS OF DOUBLE VIEW SCHOOL, CINDERFORD, 1915, with J.R. Emery, headmaster.

SOUDLEY PEACE PROCESSION, 1919.

ST STEPHENS CHURCH SUNDAY SCHOOL FETE, Cinderford, c. 1910. Another of A. Runicles' photographs.

CO-OP PENNY BANK TREAT, Cinderford, 1908. The parade which preceded the Penny Bank tea – one of Cinderford's many and fondly remembered processions. Others included the Baptists' and the Trades Processions. In this picture, leading the parade (left) is S. Rowlinson of the boot and shoe shop.

CORONATION DAY CELEBRATIONS AT LYDNEY, 1911.

CROWD AT NEWNHAM, c. 1911. A bit of a mystery, this photograph. It is one of a set of four, one of which shows the band (no doubt the Newnham Band) marching up the street. I have been unable to find anyone who remembers the occasion. In one of the other photographs a couple of women are wearing what looks like the regalia of Good Templars, so this may have been a temperance demonstration. On the left: Victoria Hotel, saddler's Shop (Joseph Moss), True Heart Inn.

ANOTHER MYSTERY. Thought to be at Recreation Ground, Parkend. The group includes M. Edwards, J. Turley, H. Edwards, Stodger Morgan, but the occasion is unknown. Note the squashed bucket the one man is holding, which may provide a clue to the mystery for somebody.

WESTBURY FARMERS AT A ROOT, FRUIT AND GRAIN SOCIETY EVENT, 1920. Back row: C.H. Bullett, J. Stephens, S. Hooper, S. Cowles, A.R. Ebborn, E. Hill, W. Hart, J. Mayo. Front: E. Woodman, W. Littleton, J. Vaughan, W. Bennett, A.R. Littleton.

On Wheels

'Let him that purposeth to travel, first
Begin where he was born, bred up and nurst'
Anon.

FLOAT, WAGON, AND TROLLEY AT THE CROWN, THE LEA, 1900 or earlier. A little outside our district perhaps. Loaded with cider made by Phillip Woodman of the original Junction Inn, Northwood, Westbury. Note the broad-wheeled Gloucestershire wagon, pulled by three horses, as is the trolley. Phillip Woodman (the name Woodman can be seen on the trolley) made quantities of cider which he sold to local public houses. As late as 1914 there were still more than one hundred and seventy wheelwrights in Gloucestershire; many wheelwrights were also wagon builders. Somewhere near here, on Saturday 30 October 1795, a party of Forest colliers waylaid a wagon of barley and another of wheat, which they took to feed the starving people of Drybrook.

BUTCHER'S VAN OUTSIDE OAKLE STREET HOTEL, C. 1903. Left: A.R. Littleton, the butcher, of Duni Farm, Minsterworth, and Dodger Russell. Canvas top, the flap at rear was used as a chopping board.

GOVERNESS CART – the safest of horse carriages. Usually driver and passengers sat sideways but this does not appear to be the case here; so, strictly speaking, this may not be a governess cart. When locally made there would be variation in design from district to district. Exact location not known.

GIG/TRAP, 1917 – and very smart too. Miss Olive Grindon at Jordan House, Westbury, who married J. Ambrose, wheelwright at the Weightbridge, Westbury. Motor-cycle in background.

GIG. A.R. Littleton (holding reins) with Dr Fisher at Hunt Hill, Westbury on a Sunday morning, 1920s. After surgery on Sunday mornings, it was Dr Fisher's custom to visit one of the local inns for his own particular medicine.

WAGONETTE AT THE BIRD IN HAND, CHAXHILL, c. 1920. Alfred Ayland (standing at front of wagonette) ran a passenger service and carrier service from Westbury to Gloucester via Rodley. Later, one son, Alfred, ran a passenger service with a motor bus, and another, Archibald, had a motor lorry. By the horses, Fred Sergeant. Note: this carriage has a centre pole instead of shafts. The small front wheels allowed a better lock and turning.

WAGONETTE WITH COLEFORD CHILDREN.

HARRY GRINDLE OF CINDERFORD with his carriage and pair near the Greyhound at Elton, c. 1916. Both his sons followed him in the same line of business but with motor vehicles. At the horses' heads, Arthur Bell. The carriage was probably about to take a bride to church.

YOUNG LADY WITH BICYCLE — note dress guard on rear wheel. The young man is sitting on a tumbril or dung cart. This type of cart could be tipped; it was still in general use in the 1950s, until the tractor finally usurped the horse.

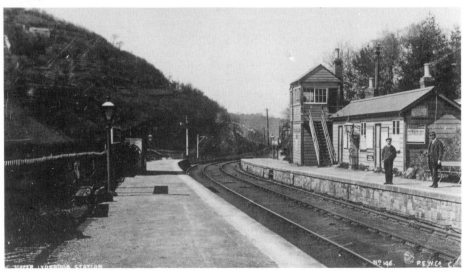

UPPER LYDBROOK STATION. Opened for freight August 1874; for passengers September 1875. Closed for freight January 1956; for passengers July 1929. Return fare from here to Bristol was two shillings and sixpence in 1894.

GRANGE COURT STATION, c. 1912. Designed by Brunel, with additions in 1855 for Hereford line (foreground). Back left: the stationmaster's house. Opened (South Wales line) in 1851 (Hereford Line, June 1855), the station was closed in November 1964 and later demolished.

NEWNHAM STATION, c. 1909. Opened 19 September 1851 (S. Wales line); addition of bay line to Forest, 1907 (the Forest rail–motor can be seen in bay). The passenger service to the Forest started August 1907 and by April 1908 it was running to the new Cinderford Station and as far as Drybrook Halt, which closed for passengers in 1930. Service for passengers to Cinderford closed November 1958. The station closed November 1964.

CINDERFORD NEW STATION, c. 1902. Opened July 1900 – G.W.R. train from Newnham started 1908. Closed for passengers, 1958; for freight, 1967. Demolished 1968. Mrs Runicles and children in foreground. The photograph was taken by A. Runicles, whose daughter, pictured here, loaned the photograph.

WHITECROFT STATION c. 1910, looking north. Midland Railway and Severn & Wye Joint Railway Station opened September 1875 (second platform added 1897). Closed to passengers July 1929, to freight October 1967.

W.D. WALKLEY'S LORRY.

WINTLES' BREWERY LORRY, outside a public house the name of which is barely discernible, but it looks like The Clytha Arms. Note the solid rubber tyres.

MUNN'S GARAGE, CINDERFORD, July 1920. The photograph includes: Stanley Wilce and his Swift motor-car, Victor Mundy with motor-cycle and sidecar, Mr & Mrs Mundy snr. in back of motor-car, Co-op delivery lorry, the first Cinderford ambulance, and a Shell delivery lorry.

SECTION ELEVEN

People

'What is in a man's heart is on his face,
and is shortly written all over him'
                                        Irving Batcheller

WILLIAM AYLAND AND HIS WIFE with their sons, Alfred and Asgill, Westbury. William Ayland ran a carrier service to Gloucester via Rodley. Alfred was also a carrier and the last to work the Westbury corn-mill. All of Alfred's children and grandchildren had Christian names which began with the letter A.

JOE EDWARDS AND CHARLIE MORGAN, PARKEND, between 1910–1920. Church and the Fountain public house in background.

FAMILY GROUP AT POUND COTTAGE, Minsterworth, c. 1900. Far right, Mr Mitchell.

KING FAMILY AT HILL FARM, Lydney, 1897. Seated: Mr and Mrs Edward King and daughter. In front, left: Ernest King who later farmed at Flaxley.

A. RUNICLES WITH HIS MOTHER, A VISITOR AND HIS CHILDREN, early twentieth century. Mr Runicles took several of the photographs which appear in this book, but his wife took this one.

AT WESTBURY COURT, 15 August 1905. Front centre in white hat: Miss Cecilia Wemyss – note her wristwatch, which must have been very modern.

GRANDCHILDREN OF ISAIAH YOUNG OF FLAXLEY at school in Blaisdon, 1920s.

HOLDER FAMILY AT FLAXLEY MILL.

PICNIC IN THE FOREST — and in fine style. The young man in cap appears to be eating a boiled egg. What wonderful hats the ladies are wearing; their costume gives an idea of the date.

FOUR JOVIAL GENTLEMEN AT WHITEHOUSE FARM, ADSETT, WESTBURY, c. 1922. Left to right: Henry Jackson, who built the present Junction Inn and was the first licensee (he was also a dealer in fruit); Dr Fisher, for many years medical practitioner at Westbury; Ernest Hill, farmer of same parish; and Cecil Miller, a traveller for Godsell's Brewery (Stroud).

JESSE KNIGHT, shepherd at Awre, 1946. It could be 1906 or even earlier, which just shows the amount of change in the last forty years, compared to the previous forty or even eighty. Here we have a man of sturdy character and can only regret the passing of such men.

DR. NICCOL FREDERICK SEARANCKE. Medical practitioner at Mitcheldean 1883–1931. Died 23rd March 1931.

AT TUTNALLS. The farmer in centre with straw hat is James Saunders.

JOHN POPE OF COLEFORD, shoemaker and Town Crier. Born 18th May 1788 in the parish of Rodborough, Stroud; died 26th May 1873 at Coleford. He was Coleford Town Crier from some time between 1859 and 1863 until at least 1870. He made both shoes and clogs and was referred to as a cordwainer, the older name for shoemaker. His son, Joseph, was a tailor and shoemaker at Cinderford, and John Pope's grandson (A.W. Pope) and great-grandson (A.J. Pope) were shoemakers at Cinderford.

EBENEZER TYNDALE AND HIS SISTER, PRISCILLA. c. 1905. They had a sweet shop in Church Road, Cinderford. Legend has it that they were descendants of William Tyndale, translator of the Bible. This is doubtful, because little or nothing was known of William Tyndale's family. And yet, they look as if they could well be descendants of the martyr.

E.J. FLOOKS of the White Horse, Mitcheldean, with his daughter, c. 1906.

JAMES BALDWIN, manager of East Slad Colliery, Ruardean Woodside and his grandson, Fred Hale who later had a sawmill at Nailbridge.

TWO MEN OF AWRE WITH A VISITOR. Left, Prestbury Awre; right, Bob Jenner, both farmers. Prestbury Awre was at the Red Hart Inn 1929–49. There have been Awres at Awre for centuries, and it is debatable whether they gave the place its name or if it gave them their's. And like Jesse Knight they are drinking cider; Awre the home of the famous Hagloe Crab, being a place where cider would be the natural drink.

A WEDDING SOMEWHERE IN THE FOREST (probably Coleford district), C. 1900 – and a pleasant way to conclude.

PHOTOGRAPH CREDITS

R. Adams ● G. Aldridge ● C. Awre ● S. Awre ● A. Ayland ● A. Bayliss ● J. Belcher
M. Bickerton ● T. Brain ● Bream R.F.C. ● R. Bullock ● D. Butt ● A. Cadogan
C. Cadogan ● Cinderford R.F.C. ● E. Coley ● M. Cooper ● Mrs. Davies ● P. Davis
Dean Forest Newspapers ● C. French ● Mrs. Gibson ● Glos. Newspapers
N. Gould ● P. Green ● J. Hale ● D. Harvey ● Mrs. Harvey ● Mrs. Hill ● O. Holford
Dr. Holland ● Mrs. Jayne ● D. King ● M. Lambert ● J. Littleton ● Mrs. Luker
Lydney R.F.C. ● Lydney Town Band ● E. Olivey ● Mrs. Parry ● H. Phelps ● A. Pope
J. Powell ● Mrs. Priest ● J. Saunders ● M. Sellick ● V. Shingles ● H. Trigg
L. Tuffley ● B. Walker ● F. Webb ● F. Wherrett ● Mrs. Williams ● N. Young

and W. Austin for photographic work